Born to be Wild
Little Marmots

Anne Royer

Words that appear in the glossary are printed in
boldface type the first time they occur in the text.

GARETH**STEVENS**
GS
PUBLISHING
A WRC Media Company

Staying Warm Next to Mom

A female marmot carries her unborn babies inside her body for five weeks. A few days before her babies are born, she moves to the bottom of her **burrow** to stay alone. Mother marmots do not want to be around other marmots when giving birth. So that she will be left alone, the female marmot closes up the burrow's entrance with hay and dirt. She will give birth to her babies in the dark on a bed made of hay.

A marmot's babies are born in a burrow she has dug into a grassy mountain slope. Marmots usually live in areas so high on mountains that trees cannot grow.

What do you think?

What are a marmot's babies called?

a) marmottons

b) baby marmots

c) marmitons

3

A marmot's babies are simply called baby marmots.

At birth, baby marmots are blind and hairless and weigh only 1 ounce (30 grams). They are so **fragile** that their mothers leave them only for very short periods of time, usually to eat. When a mother marmot must leave, she covers her babies with hay so they don't get cold, and their body temperatures don't fall. Baby marmots drink their mother's milk for about two months. When the babies leave their burrows, they discover fresh grass to eat.

Female marmots do not have a **litter** every year. They give birth once every other year and have two to four babies in each litter.

By the time little marmots are about ten days old, they have tripled their birth weight. They are also starting to grow short, dark hair on their bodies.

When baby marmots are about two weeks old, they are less fragile than they were at birth. Their mothers no longer have to keep them warm all the time.

At one month of age, the marmots' fur has grown, their eyes are wide open, and their front teeth, called **incisors**, have started to grow. Soon it will be time for the baby marmots to **venture** outside the burrow.

First Time Out

Little marmots do not wait until they are outside to play together. They start doing somersaults while they are still inside their burrows. Little by little, they venture down the long corridors of the burrow that lead to the outside. When they are about six weeks old, they will finally go outdoors and begin to explore these new surroundings, where they will now live, eat, and play.

What do you think?

How long do young marmots stay with their families?

a) two years

b) six months

c) five to six years

Little marmots stay close to their burrows on the first day outside. If a baby marmot tries to go too far, its mother brings it back, holding her baby gently between her teeth.

Young marmots stay with
their families for two years.

A marmot family consists of two parents, the baby
marmots born in spring, and their older brothers and
sisters. A family group usually has about ten animals.
They all live together in the same burrow. They also
share a common **territory** with other families, forming
a **colony** of marmots.

Little marmots
are always willing
to fight, and they
especially like
boxing. To box,
marmots stand
on their back legs
while resting on
their tails.

When they first go outside the burrow, little marmots stay close together near the entrance. They will wait a few days before playing in the grass.

Every day, a baby marmot becomes bolder and ventures a little farther away from its burrow. When it meets another marmot, it touches its nose to the other marmot's throat to say hello.

A Beautiful Summer Day

Early in the morning, a marmot pokes its head out of the burrow. After quickly cleaning its coat, it moves a short distance away from the burrow and starts eating grass. Meanwhile, another marmot has come out of the burrow. Very soon, the entire colony will be eating its first meal of the day. Marmots do not drink, so they like to eat when the grass is still wet with dew. During summer, they will gulp down huge amounts of food each day. Marmots must build up a lot of fat in their bodies to live on during the long, snowy winters.

Marmots are **rodents** and, like all rodents, have long incisors. They use these teeth to cut off the tender grasses they like to eat. Rodents' incisors grow all through their lives. To keep their incisors from getting too long, marmots constantly rub one against another.

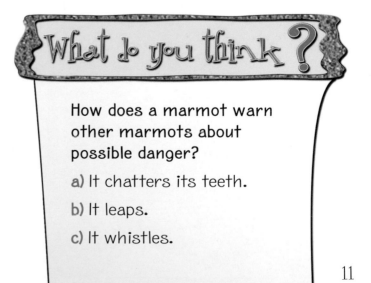

What do you think?

How does a marmot warn other marmots about possible danger?

a) It chatters its teeth.

b) It leaps.

c) It whistles.

To warn others of danger, a marmot whistles.

Even when a marmot is busy eating, it frequently raises its head for a quick look around its territory. If the marmot sees a shadow or hears a strange noise, it stands up on its back legs, raises its head, and whistles to warn the other marmots. They all stop what they are doing and rush to the nearest burrows to hide.

In late morning, marmots like to sunbathe. To be safe, they sit near the entrances to their burrows.

Marmots have fun sunbathing in a group. To get rid of bugs, however, marmots take dirt baths!

The golden eagle is a marmot's worst enemy. Eagles usually attack the youngest marmots or those that are sick.

Marmots whistle to communicate with each other. One of the sounds they make warns other marmots in the colony when an eagle or some other enemy has been seen.

Games are not just for little marmots. Adult marmots like to box, too.

Sleepy Heads

As fall approaches, a marmot must get ready for its long winter sleep. All of the marmots in a family work together to prepare for the cold, snowy season. They have to dig a new winter burrow or improve their summer burrow. The marmots have spent the spring and summer eating and growing as fat as possible. Their winter burrow must be big enough and deep enough to fit an entire family of much fatter marmots. Once the marmots are inside the burrow and have closed the entrance with dirt, they will not come out again for six months. They will **hibernate**, or sleep, until spring.

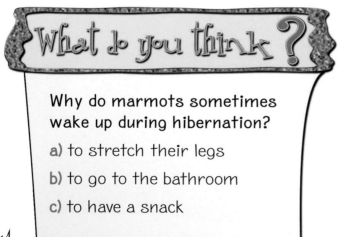

What do you think?

Why do marmots sometimes wake up during hibernation?

a) to stretch their legs

b) to go to the bathroom

c) to have a snack

The closer winter gets, the fatter marmots grow! They must eat as much as possible before they hibernate. During fall, they are also very busy picking grass, which they let dry in the sun. Marmots use dried grass to cover the bottoms of their winter burrows.

During hibernation, marmots sometimes wake up to go to the bathroom.

During their six months of hibernation, marmots wake up only four or five times. They get up to go to the bathroom, using a room in the burrow that they dug just for this purpose. Marmots spend the rest of the winter sleeping. They do not even eat. They can survive because of the extra fat they added to their bodies when they were eating a lot.

The thicker the snow covering the burrow, the warmer the marmots stay. Snow acts like a winter coat, **insulating** the burrow from the cold.

In winter, marmots sleep curled up in a ball on beds of warm, dry grass.

No matter what the weather is like, marmots always wake up in early April. Scientists do not know what kind of alarm clock tells the marmots that it's time to pop out of their burrows.

Spring Is Here!

In spring, marmots wake up from their long hibernation. They quickly begin to open up the entrances to their burrows and dig tunnels through the snow that still covers the mountains. Even in spring, the snow on a mountain can be very deep, and marmots cannot find one blade of grass to snack on. While they hibernated, the marmots already lost half of their body weight, but they will need to keep living off of their fat reserves for a few more weeks.

When marmots first come outside in spring, they use any bit of sunlight to warm up. When there is no grass to eat, marmots sometimes eat snow to get the water they need.

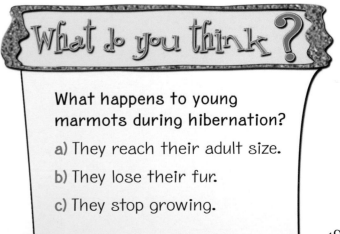

What do you think?

What happens to young marmots during hibernation?

a) They reach their adult size.

b) They lose their fur.

c) They stop growing.

During hibernation, young marmots stop growing.

Marmots do not grow while they hibernate. Because of this delay, a marmot reaches its adult size only after it is three or four years of age. When they are one year old, young marmots usually are only about 12 inches (30 centimeters) long, half the size of an adult marmot.

At two years old, marmots start to take long trips. One day, they will not return to their family burrows. They will be ready to start their own families in another colony.

As soon as the snow has melted, it's time for spring-cleaning! Marmots fix up their summer burrows and dig other, smaller, burrows for safety.

A marmot's first concern after coming out of hibernation is not looking for food but visiting with the other members of its colony.

Two weeks after waking up, it's already time for **mating season**. Marmots usually mate underground in their burrows.

Marmots are **mammals**. Most marmots live on grassy slopes high in the mountains of the northern **hemisphere**. In the wild, marmots live an average of ten years. An adult marmot weighs between 7 and 15 pounds (3 and 7 kilograms), depending on the season.

Marmots are members of the squirrel family and are related to ground squirrels, prairie dogs, and chipmunks. The most common marmot in North America is the woodchuck.

Even though a marmot has a very short neck, it can turn its head easily.

An adult marmot is about 23 inches
(60 cm) long, not including its bushy tail.

A marmot's tiny
ears are almost
entirely hidden
under its coat.

Marmots have small rounded
eyes. Although they do not see
clearly, they can see wide areas.

A marmot's most
developed sense
is smell.

Marmots have short
powerful legs and long
claws that help them dig.

GLOSSARY

burrow — a hole in the ground that is dug by an animal to be used as its home

colony — a group of the same kind of animal or plant living or growing together

fragile — easily broken or hurt

hemisphere — half of Earth's surface, divided either north and south or east and west

hibernate — to spend the winter in an inactive state, such as sleeping or resting

incisors — sharp front teeth that animals use for cutting food

insulating — covering, lining, or surrounding with a material that helps keep cold, heat, electricity, or sound from passing through

litter — a group of young animals born at the same time to the same mother

mammals — warm-blooded animals that have backbones, give birth to live babies, feed their young milk from the mother's body, and have skin that is usually covered with hair or fur

mating season — the time of year when male and female animals join to produce offspring

rodents — animals with large incisors, such as rats and beavers

territory — an area of land that animals occupy and defend

venture — to take on the risks and dangers of an activity

Please visit our web site at: www.garethstevens.com
For a free color catalog describing Gareth Stevens Publishing's list of high-quality books and multimedia programs, call 1-800-542-2595 (USA) or 1-800-387-3178 (Canada). Gareth Stevens Publishing's fax: (414) 332-3567.

Library of Congress Cataloging-in-Publication Data

Royer, Anne.
    [Petite marmotte. English]
    Little marmots / Anne Royer. — North American ed.
        p. cm. — (Born to be wild)
    ISBN 0-8368-4439-4 (lib. bdg.)
    1. Marmots—Infancy—Juvenile literature. I. Title. II. Series.
QL737.R68R68 2005
599.36'6—dc22   2004058188

This North American edition first published in 2005 by
Gareth Stevens Publishing
A WRC Media Company
330 West Olive Street, Suite 100
Milwaukee, Wisconsin 53212 USA

First published in 2003 as *La petite marmotte* by Mango Jeunesse, an imprint of Editions Mango, Paris, France.

Picture Credits [top = t, bottom = b, left = l, right = r]
Bios: C. Barbançon 5(tr); C. Ruoso 5(tl), 12(b), 21; F. Berndt 7; D. Bringard 12(t); K. Wothe 13(tr); V. Fournier 15; R. Valarcher 18; H. Ausloos 20(t). Colibri: Ch. Simon title page, 13(bl), 22(l); Negro-Cretu back cover, 5(b); D. Magnin cover, 3; B&C Baranger 8, 9(t), 13(br); C. Balcœur 9(b); Pouyfourcat 16(b). Sunset: G. Lacz 2, 4, 10, 22-23; L. Bertrand 16(tl); C. Simon 17; B. Simon 20(b).

English translation: Muriel Castille
Gareth Stevens editor: Barbara Kiely Miller
Gareth Stevens art direction: Tammy West

Printed in the United States of America

1 2 3 4 5 6 7 8 9 09 08 07 06 05